SEMBLANCES
1962 - 1971

SEMBLANCES
1962 - 1971

Vincent Barrett Price

SEMBLANCES
1962 - 1971

Vincent Barrett Price

THE SUNSTONE PRESS
SANTA FE, NEW MEXICO

ISBN 0 - 913270 - 64 - 4

To the editors of

Albireo Quarterly
Beloit Poetry Journal
Discourse: A Review of the Liberal Arts
Dust
Grande Ronde Review
Encanto
New York Quarterly
Poetry Review
Seared Eye
Solo Press
South Dakota Review
Southwest Review
Today
Wild Dog

the author makes grateful acknowledgement.

The illustrations in this volume are by Rini Price, a painter, illustrator and craftsperson; and by James P. Rini, an artist and political cartoonist for THE NEW MEXICO INDEPENDENT. Both live in Albuquerque.

Manufactured in the United States of America

For

Rini, Roland, Robert, Michael and Christina.
With special love to Edith, Vincent and Mary.

TABLE OF CONTENTS

PARCELS FROM HOME

FIVE THOUSAND THREE HUNDRED
AND TWENTY FIVE WOLVES

Sally and Gwen mount rats
over the doll house hearth.
Shrunken snowmen
hang by their lips.

Moonpaths, skinned
from the doddering sea,
inflame seedy stenos
with kissing-sweet breath.

The Smithsonian is
the last wilderness left.
Nostalgia is not a kind burden.

The last lichen was ambushed
at dawn in Vermont.
The bounty was 25 cents.

Wolves are hunted by aeroplane in Alaska for $50 a pelt. In November, 1969, there were only 5,325 left within the continental limits of the United States.

LESS THAN WE BARGAINED FOR

To die statuesque
for sentiment
in a village square,

limestone, sun
hewn by bare knuckles
in well-phrased,
older worlds . . .

In those days, to die
was a gesture
of gentility, good breeding,
better than widows
or wheat.

Nowadays, to die
means to malfunction
and we tend to resent
shoddy goods.

HARD CORE

And I ask myself, why do I strive
for bed-warm meadows, for thunder, firm light,
for crisp-linen winds to be served with my coffee,
bare ocean and thighs, or fall upon fledgling kites,
tearing them down, limb from limb, from the sky?
Why do I keep aloof as I do
from somersaults, soaps, smutty bowties, and sod cellars,
or cheer when strippers slap mustard and relish
all over our jiggling, slug-soft minds?

Because, it's really quite simple, I stammer, sweat fog,
and panther about in fat pants, painstakingly out of the blue,
inspiring fibs, janitorial moods, and quack killers.
Because, where virtue's concerned, I'd prefer
Pteranodons gulping high over head
to an Oz without cheesy witches,
and would trust, above all,
fingernail growth, heat rashes, trap doors,
and sailboats with stores for a forty year cruise.

BEST FOOT FORWARD

. . . and there is that perfect feather you found
not four yards from where we throw darts.

But what of the rest
—the illegible squalling of so many siamese souls,
the jibberish
geometrically progressed,
crescendoing
through the men's room, the president's office,
the faculty lounge,
through the office of Simon the butcher:
there's a calendar there
with photos of Venice,
Berlin, Vera Cruz in the rain, and Constantinople,
but Simon can't read the captions really,
or won't.

It's neo-Byzantium, mosaical!
the domino theory
all laid out on the wainscot
of Bedlam's barber shop:
rational units, arranged to equate,
grouted with rank iridescence and dandruff
depicting:
five suffragettes, Abe Lincoln,
lounging with bull dogs in bowlers puffing cigars
an hour before sun up
on *le grande jatte.*

And you and I
poke through the gala
in basic black,
our shoes
deliberately skuffed.

---

*Houston beach party. Apollo XI. Seurat pinpointing the problem but
it doesn't pop. Why couldn't they have left us behind?!*

16

POSITIVE MILLSTONES

No risks. No risks at all
—only the crossbow, abacus, usury,
and the wily Macedonian wedge
(put to good use by Bronco Nagurski
and Yalies with quilted cocks);
not the *moon,* surely?

Why, back then
the invention of gunpowder
was as grisly to them
as the aerosol bomb is to us
and everyone had the sense to foresee
that mousetraps would, eventually,
fall into the hands of the Inquisition.

They didn't care then;
they can't afford to now.

Horizon has slipped
rare Spanish Fly,
all the way from Cathay,
into our jellied consummé
and we bray; Titanic's curse
or Titania's, Horizon always
arises with us in her eyes.

Who *will* be the first
to plant spikes in those craters
and cover them over with papier mache?
There's not a sage alive who can bear to resist
the thought of a succulent Snipe fillet.

---

*After Armstrong's great leap forward. A "positive milestone" in the
history of human inquiry.*

17

LONGEVITY
for Howard Estberg*

Hebe, 73,
survives in fat and trees,
in the shadows of her turbans,
her Saks Fifth Avenue folds.
All her daffodils died
of milk of magnesia and gin.
Her hat boxes smell
of black strap molasses.
With purpose
she saves her urine,
fogs her glasses
over crocks of Manchu tea
and finds
ontological flaws
in her Persian rugs.
Her teeth are teak veneered.
The world doesn't care
if Hebe throws dice
or lustily snears
at giant male mice.
She hasn't washed in 15 years.
Her bannisters are spotless.
It's hard to imagine
the state of her crotch.

Leo, 50 to 95,
is hard to say.
He hides in his eyes,
excessively sane.
Too proud
to be unhappy,
too smart to die
of placebos and grief,
he uses his heart
as others use tents,
or machetes,
or days by the sea:
he know infirmity
breeds respect,
the audience loves
an elegant loser.
Leo survives
by his cunning fate,
his restless charm,
his alarming,
defenseless
self-respect.

Howard, 86, however, abides.
His clocks have no eyes.
Howard sees through time
as others see
through the bottoms of crystal steins.
Howard
honors the world
with delight;
with curiosity
has he honored his life.
Be it chocolates in bed
and Mickey Spillane,
or Indonesian pagodas,
Howard knows
good times come
one at a time.
"Time! Time! Time!

Never enough, you know.
If I don't die, I'll do it."
Howard wouldn't make time to die; besides,
his clocks are absent minded.

Wendy, deceased,
had nothing to save.
She didn't survive,
hide or abide. She paid.
Pegasus, pixies, nordic knights,
Mozart, Alice, her passion for Pan,
for apricots, snow and hopeless grails
—her life was too much for old age;
rather, I mean, her person
meant less than her vision
and she tried to see for the world.
Hebe and Leo
they're quaint,
more than that really
but harmlessly more:

honest, eccentrically bold,
not in any sense old,
but ruthlessly old nonetheless.
They
are kept to themselves.
It's their place
to ward off the world
and gloat. God knows
they've earned it.
But Wendy,
she secluded herself
at the age of 8;
she couldn't wait
how many years
to be honest.
Wendy retired
into the truth
when everyone's busy
saving their youth

for those endlessly
rainy days, when self
overcomes obligation.
Wendy was martyred
exactly for this:
she overcame
before it's too late,
made everyone feel
foolishly frugal.
By spending herself
all in one place,
she lived her life
as a rich anti-climax
while the rest were banking that death is.

Howard, however, abides.
He saved his life
for his lifetime.

---

*With gratitude for his 86th birthday. It was learned that Wendy
died in a mental institution the day I picked a Blackeyed Susan from
the front lawn of her "Nopalitas."*

DOCTOR DENTON WAS A FREUDIAN

Monday morning:

Lubed with espresso, in Eskimo tweeds
sculpted by know-it-all, hazardous Greeks
from herringbone bought, for a song, on a lark
at a wholesome Goodwill where they still

deal in dickies, hoodwinks and spats,
snug as a fox with no shadow, a ghost
bundled up in chimney smoke and fallen leaves,
I settle over the hopes of the day, blessed,

by the chivalrous genius of nightcaps,
hot chocolate and four-poster beds, with a chilly,
taut, barebottom dawn to be warm on—warm
as the businesslike nest between us each night

where shady Lawrence,
our polar black arctic cat, is hatching a plot
to unionize hares for a franchise in fur
so birds won't fly south in the winter.

New autumn in my $2.49 ice blue Harris Tweeds.

22

DECISIONS, DECISIONS

If,
in a Lennox Avenue flat,
upholstered in rust, flamingoes, swank bamboo,
the conquering Chink
executioner said,
either your wife,
your child,
or you,
why would I,
the only survivor,
my life so full of last stands
and companions
I've saved myself from
without hesitation
say me?
Would it be
the same if he said,
either all the cats,
every last otter,
primrose and boa,
or you?
No.
Do unto others
is only for lovers.
That's why
the Cross was no choice.

NINE TO FIVE

I am and I am not what I seem.
I seem to be both and neither.
I know but I do not understand.

I want but I do not desire.
I speak but I do not tell.
I lie but I do not commit error.

I hold yes and no together.
They cannot tear me apart.
I know but I do not understand.

"A man is what he thinks about all day long."—Emerson

CHRISTMAS LICENSE

When you come to our house this Christmas,
open the little jars.
You are free to have whatever you find:

      the shadows of eagles in cellophane sacks;
a stack of arthritic rain;
      all your thoughts on a micro-dot;
a slab of the Sundance Sea;
      Goethe's bad breath over sensible gossip and gooseberry wine;
a primer on Mayan subjunctives;
      that wind the first morning you broke from her bed;
Long John Silver's confidence.

You are free to have whatever you find.
Our pleasure, indeed. But please,
be kind to Jesus and Jude, look for the truth,
take liberties with your mind.

MERRY VICTORIOUS

I had her WHOLE body on my back.
We piggyback galloped up Nicholas Beach
and she never *once* grabbed for my throat

—my sister, the lith Brunhilda,
8-year-old tough, and new with fun,
urgently merry,
dogmatic
her elders have called it,
tyrannical fun.

Oh, she'll hold your hand, if you don't ask her,
whisper of infinite things while you're reading the paper
—this strenuous, sea-cozy self
in such a serious body,
this gifted explorer, piano deserter,

this genius
for whom mountain-stones
burst from high tides, heavy
with moonquartz and crystal, especially for her.

Victorious child!
Self-cultured classic!
"So much of me," she shouts, "and all so luscious."

She will be my best friend before I am forty,
will confide with me hectic dilemmas at overtime coffees, but
amaze her own way through her life, and will

have probably salvaged mine
by the time I'd otherwise be
too indulgently wise to care.

And *I*
had her WHOLE body on my back:
Atlas, St. Christopher, Ol' St. Nick—what a load! My sister,

arch patron prophet, *she*
transforms, she loves
wind into light, light into flesh, her mind into the weather,
responsible first
to her self-respect: it's her pleasure

to which the world will adapt
to enjoy itself with her.
She wouldn't have anything less;
her smile an infallible omen.

In celebration of my 30th birthday, a grateful admiration of my sister, Mary Victoria Price.

LOCKJAWS AJAR

I said *this*
in passing.
And she told him
I'd meant *that*
emphatically instead.
Then he
got mad at him
because he didn't know
and did it anyway, even though
he had no way of knowing
that he'd done it.
And now I must explain
what she didn't say I said
for I would contradict myself
if I denied it.

What comes of confiding banter.

WREN GRAY

. . . like wolfpup down
this dawn
where not a sound
but wetness
muffled in the soil
like light
in grays and browns
has changed this town
to nordic plains
where fur and claw
and bells on sleighs
dismiss me
by way of hazy
stones and hay
stacked sensual as days
piled on each other
reconciled to touch
voluptuous
as the light
that lies between us . . .

Mind gust, hunting for slippers.

EXHIBIT A

Rocks rub off.
Leaves smear.
Clouds cake under my nails.
Even the desert skips a space.
And yet,

I am certain
windows are crypts
swarming with riches and risks,
to be taken by force,
without shame or recourse
to vain postulations.

       ***

       Don't I smell smoke?
My fat!
       It's on fire!

       ***

I cherish only
what I don't know.
I'm a glutton
for bare essentials.

I put boulders on my tongue.
I have seen the wind thaw.
Still, I am
a cheap thrill to myself.
I've put off fraud for such a long time,
surprises now come with instructions.

The morning after too much applause.

EXHIBIT B

Head like a blistered heel.

Eyes like matted fur.

Sky slips from the earth
like old meringue
after a twelve-hour day
in the Fey Apparatus.

Carps flopping to death on spotless decks.

Surplus fanatics.

Tacticians condemned to my brain.

Give me room please! A little air!
It's all over folks. Head on home.
Not a morsel has gone undetected.
There's no mopping up to be done.

I am no longer
elsewhere,
or anywhere
—like a dear dead friend,
I exist like that
just inside me.

_____

After an insulting political victory.

WORLD HURT

We share everything—all of us
—it can't be helped.
We even share ourselves.
As Crusoe shared his island
before good Friday's proud escape,
we share the air,
the bed, the marigolds,
Ashanti, Mars, and photosynthesis.
And we are
no more or less alone
for what we share.
And just because
you can only know
as much of me as I can know,
minus what I choose
kindly not to give, or can't bestow,
it does not mean
we do not share each other.
We share meaning
with Andromeda, we do not know her;
and we are
no more
or less alone
for what we share.

What's the difference then?

What's the difference if we say,
in all good faith and pleasure,
"I share my life with you. It's yours, it's mine,
it can't be helped—you know it";
if we say in rapt agreement, "Yes, I know, I know",
and sharing even that
stare off around the room we share,
no more or less alone?
What *is* the difference, then,
that can't be helped,
if we say, with gentle thanks,
"Yes, I know you know. I *know* it",
while out of deference to the obvious
we implore below our breaths,
"But only *I* can know the difference
—don't you know?"

32

ITEM ONE

Observed in a six-story corduroy cuspidor:
A.   In a lather on top,

elastic clouds
snap
and chew
            into the summits
            of dimpled-raw hills
where
      executive yogas
snuggle into their woes,
celebrant stones
                  kicked up stairs
                  abating the known
in a beefy communion
                        with zeros: their brains,
bulging
            over the clouds,
furrowed
            and steaming
            like waists
            freshly sauteed
in a size too small.

B.   On the bottom,

holy pathologists
strut and grunt
methodically
                  pinpointing
                  girls
as they pluck
            numbers and lines
            from votive
slide rules
            flopping and messy
in stingy backyards
where the sun
            is slopped
            into the wash,
            the news

crackles
  like cockroaches
  crushed,
bruised water sags
in kidney pools,
     vaginal symbols
     are sore
inner tubes
   where, at last,
   fatted fathers
come to sow,
    stroking in tempo to
    rattlesnake
    anthems, radio clocks,
counting down as they add
       new notches
onto their cocks,
    coming like fish
    gushing
    through sieves,
    nodding off
with approval
   as deathcounts increase,
strained
   through the backdoor screen.

C. Stuck to the sides,

an oily montage of pottery trees,
of red hot, wrought iron rockers,
little red wagons, expedient bees,
moony park benches,
      Rhett Butler,
faces like hoods
    and the damned
    devoured by edges;
a squalor of yawns,
      hemophiliac laws,
of hampsters and children, comfort's
debris,
    the flypaper heavens

seductively
glib,
     a bib for Implacable Abdomen Rex.

D.   Imposed from above,
at 8:35,
an impartially vague,
             wise
             formica swab,
dripping with ivy,
corns and hair,
big as a stinger
at ten thousand X,
         probing along
in a gusto
       of huffing
       and pouting, routing out
       sources, sanctum-sanctorums
—heroic
    redeemer, reformer,
    master
house cleaner,
       embryo
       tenured
       or soft
with old scripts,
         absorbing
         like shitting
in reverse
    till it gluts
    with a final
vast-sucking gasp
       then departs
       satisfied,
at 9:48,
    that everything's set
    for the next matinee.

Western Civ. II

RAW SCORE

I pinch up an inch of darkness,
here.
Presto! The edge of my skin
disappears;
I see it start
—frost
as it grows through the eye,
congealed aromas, gristly dews,
a broth of beautyspots
sprayed on a griddle,
uneasy as moss
as it puddles,
as bales of gills,
harsh
as alphabet blocks,
as nostrils in jars
of creamy jade.

An impression in the spirit of Monet. The light in grid 401-Dhb, left hemisphere, lower fringe, cerebral cortex, at 3:47 a.m.

FEE FIE FOE FUM

I don't want to be expected to be,
supposed to be, presumed to be,
and I don't want to win first prize:
a blue ribbon grub-good citizen-middleman-simpleton-stud,
a gambler
who *gambles*
not to lose face.
I don't want to be what you want me to be:
a loser who wins what you'd like to have lost,
if losing had meant no one could win.

I want no help from competent friends
who will try to guess what I mean;
nothing to help them assume what I am;
no covey of "in" connoisseurs;
no lovers
who cannot admit that I am
literally only what I can do
and not that
till I've done it and done it again.

I am what I want:
a beast and a burden,
blurting, reverted
—amazed at the truth I commit
while aching with lies,
an appearance with nothing to hide,
skin deep as the ocean,
a mudder
favored to win
at his mind.

EXHIBIT C

Club-winged angels,
hairy snakes;
scrimshaw carved
on living bone;

chamber pots
with secret shredders;
all neuropaths
lead to home:

lined with mudheads,
shrieking bears,
the orchard raves
and guests arrive;

I autograph
my brain
like others write
their names on casts.

Beneath the I-beams
and the broken bows,
a graceful window
flows, encasing

every stalking daisy.
The orchard raves
and guests arrive;
bank and bathe,

bank and bathe.
I stitched my smile,
it left a scar.
Bank and bathe,

bank and bathe.
The guests arrive,
I sign my name
V.B. Price;

shopping carts
are full of me.
Stalin's son
did not escape.

Save the trademark
on the sun
and you will get
another one.

Jonah drowning in a lower loop. Who ordered that enema, anyway?

SAVE TSEGI?

No bruised virginity to be excused.
No hymen healed with diplomatic seals
to be opened and closed like a shutter.
No WPA to take archaic Apollo
and doctor him up, new foreskin and all.

With Tsegi there is no debate,
nothing to mitigate, exonerate
(with jell-o, tintex, or oil),
nothing to spoil, no recourse.

Eden can't be redeemed
by the Chamber of Commerce
transformed to a national park.
Of course, Tsegi, Eden, Apollo exist.
Like the ark, they are
covenants: Believe, do not touch.

No one, not even Nixon, redeems
what is cleaner than prints without fingers.
No one *can*
so condescend.

Tsegi Canyon from 900 feet up. Reality, sometimes, is a symbol for myth.

TAKE IT WHERE YOU FIND IT

Yes, I saw the fly
crash into her head,
watched as the ant
toppled over, screaming
down into his tea.

It was hopeless.

I shouted,
"Watch out! Watch out!"
But my tongue,
it so happens,
had slipped
into the pudding
just then.

It was hopeless.

(God!
the relief!
sweet freedom!
the safety, giddy escape!
of blamelessly being
just too late.)

_____

The vices of a good samaritan burdened with a cool back yard.

MUTT THOUGHTS

We've talked a damn good sainthood:
an accusitive, difficult youth,
wholly our own, safe, angelically new, out-of-step,
off-to-one-side, out-of-place,
and took the vow not to retreat.

And now, in the middle, alone,
with no other choice but to agree
with who we've proposed to become
—alone, facing Shoshone, Blackfeet, Comanche,
capture, dishonor and eating crow,
dog soldiers do
mut thoughts
waiting in place
while the rest retreat
off to one side, safe, out of place,
waiting to see if we really agree
or run to "reason why".

PUT UP OR SHUT UP

We talked again.
I told him the specifics:
trust must be a common truth, a given,
absolved and absolute,
common as sleep, as dressing, decay.
It's not a means.
It's a place,
a place to be,
not be in.

I told him I knew how it was
when Tsu Hsi farted
new legislation
under her golden skirts, that I was there,
her obedient courtier dwarf, reporting each
particular mood of scent, content, between rulings,
to rub myself calm
up and down the Imperial shin.

Know your place, I told him.
He was unconvinced.

Midnight. Scented light.
Lush, mushroom moistened chill.
An owl
stopped hooting long enough
to caugh up
Mother Titmouse's apron.
I sensed no meaning.

Something's wrong.
A terrible need to say
nothing that can be said.

Mut thoughts. Smoked tongue.
Paris peace talks. Panmunjom.
All the right words
in all the wrong places:
love, trust, truth
—they can't be used again.

I love her, he said.

Noses crunching. Mugging.
Notorious
armadillos. Ice tea,
silent as seizures.
Intimidating silence: Nagasaki,
last straws, peaches
vaporized. I'm speechless!

A glistening stupor impending through my head,
silent
as photographs, swollen glass,
as stuffing, blackheads, stopsigns and collars,
tatting, cupcakes and glands;
silent as steel swelling, sperm thudding,
abcesses spreading, as gums, hangnails,
smouldering pillows, losing your keys,
or condor shit falling on Gramercy Park.

She doesn't know what she wants, he said.
Understand your man, he said.
Women will save the planet,
complete the species, I said.
He was unconvinced.

Chronic bucolic!
Folksongs ape the folks:
bikinis; panty hose; pasties,
detergent plump; government inspected
flanks, Grade A tits; "Standing on the Corner",
auctions, stockyards, Atlantic City, buyers
in the wedding ring.
No wonder!
love, trust, truth
can't be used again.

I'm speechless!

But why
on a Monday morning,
fresh from a weekend of ruins and shrines
—R. Wetherill's grave, Chis Chilling begay,
Threatening Rock, Chaco,
Crown Point and Thoreau (as they call it, "Through")
—why is my mind like Einstein's
pipe bowl?

Mut thoughts:
In Thoreau, they call Thoreau "Through",
"Threw", "Thru"!
New lamps for old!
New places to say
old things new.
It all comes "green again", I told him,
know your place.
In Thoreau, they call Thoreau "Through".
He was unconvinced,
and dog soldiers don't shake hands.

_____

Thoreau, New Mexico

44

FUZZ GLUT
for John J. Cordova

A headful of the best   conclusions,
        a luminous, humdrumming glut,   a waste of
definitive   fuzz,   combed off the tops
        of ardently awful   lifetimes of effort   to know—
peak-a-boo, thousands   of, lifetimes   concluded
        in tough, straight to the point   immaterial   froth.

It's heady in here: seltzer numb. Excelsior!
        The substance   of froth   is space. And my
poor, porous   -proud brain   —O! arid, sputtering mush—
        a mess of spaces   conclusively   phrased,
published for all   to make use of   the effortless
        moments   of   usual lives,   unusually

moved   to know down behind   the trauma of clues
        that rise,   from the matter   of substance   and style,
to incite   heads,   full of room for   vacant
        conclusions,   to scavange
for spaces   around which to
        conclude.

_____

Quick studies in the knowledge storm.

NEW YEAR'S EVE

The wizard artisans of Colhuacan
persist in sculpting for their lords
royal davenports and deep sedans,
from single slabs
of the most
recalcitrant geographies, by hand.

In waiting rooms at Midway
crusading derelicts convene,
insisting deeper in descrepancy
their histories on passers by
(who sense in turn no evidence
impending through their lives)
and sleep all night
with their hands in the pockets
as Alexander did at Babylon.

With graphite, smoke,
and bulbous pages
I worry out my mind,
insinuate the bulk
into a perfect consequence,
presuming that desire
is the difference that it makes
—inspired by my servitude
to empty drawers, to vanished stone,
the sunshine felt at 5:08
one day when I was three,
clinging to my usefulness:
a sage and ugly hunger
inspired to achieve me.

CONGENITAL SKULLDUGGERY

Go on. You can get him.
He's a sucker. Go on,
try. Tell him the truth.
He'll be *totally* disabled.
That's right, the bushwhack
—it's his one defense.
He's impervious to frontal attack.
It's a waste of time
to stalk him in a showdown
face to face.
He won't believe it.
He must catch you from behind.
Then, just ask him.
He'll be delighted,
will turn around to meet you
back to back. That's right,
tell him *exactly*
what you're going to do
—distract him,
then plunge the sword
right through your face
and stab him in the back.

Tweedle you and tweedle me: a crash survival course for the human safari.

INSOMNIA

Candle shadow:
gulping
pupil; huge
circle;
seeing
jaws, shuddering
the ceiling.
        Crippled: captive
                         shutout, offered—not an honor
        —on my back,
                falling
up,
tossed out, inside,
sighing—toilet
        tissue
wadded garlands
        streaming
           —waving up
this magnet, mouth,
          cenote,
falling,
    dangled in
green
offerings,
      falling up
this
    shadow hole: my head!
               one pore
                  opens
as I fall,
    so
it is
    the hole I'm falling in; finally,
             sucked out, head
splashed open on
       my life—wet
light there, licentious
whites, pink
twinkle rot, thinking

fat,
   flaming: soggy sparks, sagging like
                                Aunt Cally's
bag—
     brain, knifed,
               growing
slabs, spastic
swells, prickling,
               dimpled, dripping
light, sprayed
hot-sentient
         habit mush, the lush
                      from other
                      puddled heads, electric
spew
falling in
       my open head, spilling
                 heavy on
my hand—
       hold, palming
one
most round
reluctant stone
            —a lid?
to cap my head, fill up
the falling pore?
            I dip it!
                 Dip it in
my cheek,
my brow, dip it on
my gush, my skin,
        the grease, *my* grease—brain
                             breathing through
my face, draining
up
  —flesh
brain spotted, splattered as
          if I were fried
          up in a skillet
          you'd be able to baste
          your eggs in me.

So,

I dip my head
hole over, baste
the light, snuff
the candle—but
                    the fuss, I am
                    inside, ignited now
                              closed up, smouldering
all night and smoking, choked
                         out, filled up
rising
fury-mush sealed in;
                    combustable, I bloat
                                   stopped only
by the ceiling
              where I
flutter,
         snuggled,
                 rolling, rubbed until
I am too full
to hold it in
            and pop, opened
            on my life again,
                           dripping
from my lids,
the ceiling, on my face,
                      draining
through
to spot my brain,
                obliterate
the dark
        like drops
                   of water, stars or sparks
might spread,
            too utterly,
                       to consume
some surface.

_____

Waiting for sleep, waiting for fate, waiting for some clues to take.
Dee deedee dee deedee dee.

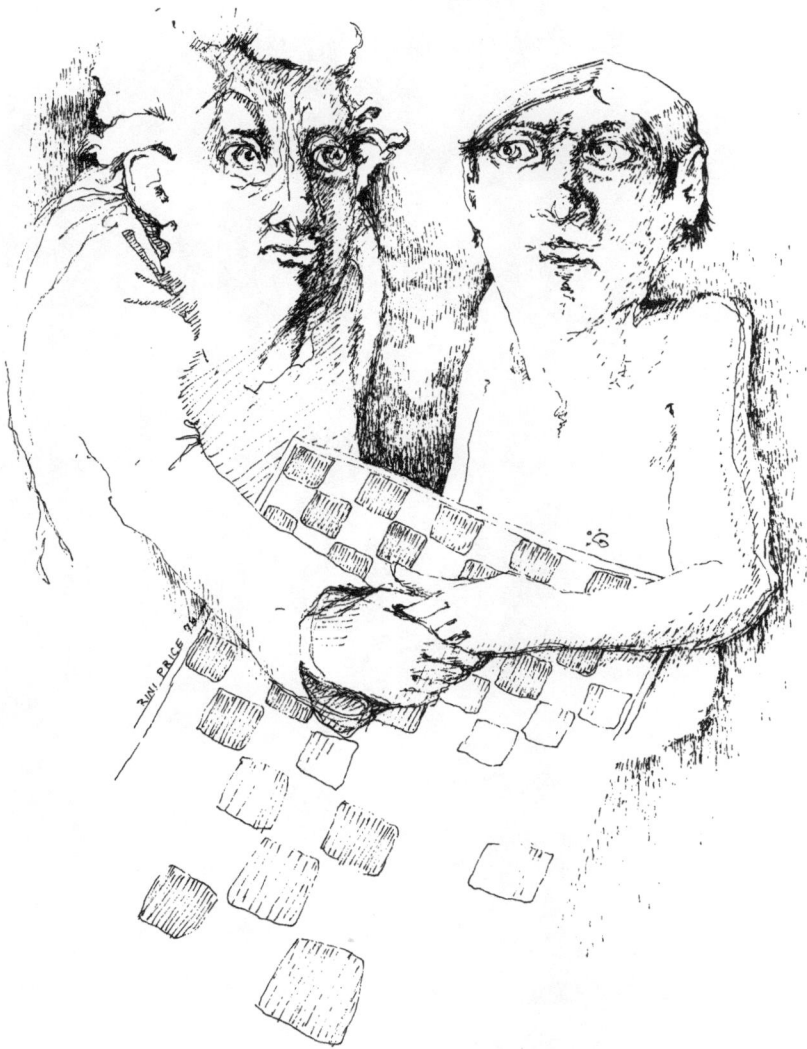

THE KEEPERS

PROPHETIC CONFESSION

Though I'm tempting as a livid pun,
homespun-handsome as Ulysses,
for your own sake, you must understand
I worship fraud, elated tragedy, as our most endearing traits;
that I stink all over with my voice, a recluse in riddles
digressed to camouflage, my face painted with temptations:
my mirror, my mirage. I've seduced ingratiating echoes
from everyone I've known, and what I've done
I've done with an inconclusive savagery.
        But even I succumb to honesty,
makeshift joy, to horror refined to elegiac tedium
and to love, like nature, that loves to hide.
And this is why I've looked for you,
luring lovelies with my face, as I am lured,
duped myself by how I look to them
but always far enough away from you
not to see you looking.

        You must understand
I've promised all my flaws away already;
that I will come to you one night, not a hero
guessed between the lies, but helpless as a madman is
unable to deceive; that I will find the urge for you alone,
redeemed from all the other lovers, in your eyes
and give you no performance, seduce from you no songs,
your body not my stage, my frenzy not your property.
        That night
we shall be for each other what our lives have said we are
—I, as always, devious, but vulnerable and free
from indiscreet ideals: the glandular cant of generations
codified to hokum; not a comfy stooge for clinical romance.
For you will have seen clear through my songs.
And we will close our eyes around each other and the dark,
trusting only what we see;
and my face will not smudge when you touch it.

THE MINISTER'S NEW CLOTHES

for Rini

> ". . . who can rule the sum total
> of the measureless?"
> —Lucretius

I've always been afraid of being terrified,
of being so possessed that I'd regret
there is no liberty from surprise.

But, moral elegance takes time—like your smile,
it catches up to me sometimes immemorial midnights later
when I'm cautious and convinced I'll be too late again to die,
to use the gift, or say goodbye; and you have warned me
with your hands, your gregorian touch, that I'm a man
who cannot know too much, nor go away without the rest.

And though we cannot mean each other, nor submit
like prophets to an insolent tranquility,
you have warned me it's our pleasure to be defied,
to be satisfied when beauty comes between us.

Love is liberty from suspicion.
The more we trust the Unforeseen,
the more we realize each other.

You are a hard new faith I must grow into
—quickly as I would the naked morning
before I can forget the stars,
if I'm to lose my way again and risk the dark,
knowing this time I'm expected.

So I will take tonight, generous as your loneliness beside me,
and rest, privileged to realize my tongue could flake away,
malignantly dissolve while dreaming safely that you'd died
on time: my final love words there, submerging with your mind.

Love is liberty from suspicion.
The more we realize the Unforeseen,
the more we trust each other.

DAWN PRINT

One crystal feather

and his hand;
her groin

savage as a pearl.

She polished an apple
on his thigh
and prepared for the day
in its reflection.

PERFECTION

Sight stashes
chips of music
in what it sees,
residue from the grinding down of self;
David's singing head and sling
pared to the whole ripe harmony of stone.

The Milky Way's
symphonic seizures
fidgit through the sky
knitting us a face
for the shedding of our scales.

A MOURNING IN RAW SILK ORANGE

Some places under the sea
are twenty feet deep in bones.
Few ever see a sloth's skull,
no one the hulk of a feather.

Bones of sperm piled in the womb:
ending is always conceiving itself.

APPLE JUNGLE

Apple
Ivory lollipop
Sweet muscle of diamond,
Orgasmic
Oval, curved as cold—ovary,
Oyster of the orchard,
Lyric shard of my illusion:

A seedless boy
Slings an apple at a nest
And the eggs
All
Fall
Down,
Breakfast for the larva.

God counts his comets
Humming home to mama
On a carrion star.

DECORATION

The wind adorned with swifts
Eating berries in its branches
In awe
He heard the healing
Of its raw, clawed trunk.

And the scar-tissue wind uprooted
Sailed across his skin
Making wakes in his illusion
To reveal then meet its twin.

Deep in the eyes of a gypsy slug
He saw his face
On the neck of the slug's twin soul.

AN EFFECT OF CURRENT FASHION

Crushing little raindrops
there is a factory for stars
and we know nothing
and cannot tell you how
in any other way:

vanishes the fly when it drinks from the vat of its body;
one beauty swills another;
the universe ferments for its own satisfaction
and prosaic we poke the delirious universe:

Old Faithful hosed to our rectums, delighting the tourists,
our vicarious eyes, in the distance
skewered on a branch with our genitals,
carefully watching the world
blowing up
through us
like firecrackers in the bowels of a squab
just eaten for lunch.

REPRODUCTIONS OF A REMINISCENCE

Her eyes
seared lemons,
the skin on her face
flapped; a wasp
with a catheter
through its thorax.

at the picnic she'd put her hand inside my shirt

Lifting her skirts
to the men at the bar,
the stitches were Persian blue.

"Formaldehyde and Snow" played on every radio

Bulls swept the streets
with bullness, scouring her face.

oysters are scarred by pearls, Hitler was in love

Licking the wind,
summer stuck to her leg.
The wind was fine and fragile,
broken by its sound. And so
she hung, noosed by her braids,
a rose stapled between her legs.

her fate took chances, gambled her away

There was nothing else
left of us to be.
A baby boy drank some perfume
and died
with the smell of a beautiful woman.

HARPY'S HEAD au gratin

Good afternoon sir.
Would you kindly take that spoon
out of my eye.

Cuddled in the slit of the sky
a thick, swirling worm.

Darling
take my head
in your hands
away from me.

The stink of burning fog,
dead mother's milk, comes
in my mouth; my mentality
limp as skin crocheted
fluffing from a damp, expectant bodice.

Starched and curled up in balloons
we tugged hankies out of auntie's ear
and mashed our centipedes to gruel.

Do stop that stirring sir.
You're premature.
Let it boil,
froth away,
till all the legs stop squirming.

My lips smack the spoon.
There's something in my throat.
Excuse me dear
I didn't know
you were in there all alone.

On my pillow
pores and puddles,
poison stinks and oils.
Bluebells on the nightstand have a rash.

Shadows in the arbor wheeze.
The wind has scraped its shins.

No, no.
I will not take the magic, dear;
it's stained,
floating with reflections
from an eye boiled down to broth
of whining pups
soiling mother's tablecloth.

Darling
take my head
it's red,
antiqued inside
like vapor spots
on coffin cushions.

I toss and turn in my skin.

I'm falling down her lap.

Under the bed,
the baby's seams are snapping.
I wish he'd stop that popping.
Welts are rising on the air.

How private she is in there,
sucking at her toes,
you'd never guess her brain has corns
but now she's putting on her hair.

The nest hums with maggots at their evening meal.

She holds my head
by the hair.
It slips
from her hand.
I step
on the hem
of my eye.

Stop poking sir.
You've broken the yolk.
Sunshine smeared across
the big bay window.
Bug-eyed, bulging
through the screen,
I sift outside too late.
The window's washed.
I squash through sunlight
in bare feet,
curled up in my eyes,
bobbing up and down,
wound up tight
in webs and underwear
I've stumbled down the air,
the spider's den,
through fallen hair,
an object of my gossip and my appetite.

THE KEEPERS

Few would know or care. Expect a horror or a prayer and you
                                  find,
always, what only your expectations know they expect.
With them, a cupid's greedy cameo.

One was a hunchback—the caricature of a wart. Born to the
                             smallest darkness,
his life was acute, but carried out behind his back.
Possessed with only the probable, frivolous with despair,
he was a wizard without a license
performing quaint, subjective alchemies on rich hoary machines;
and paid his bills like poetry under a thin, aboriginal light;
and drank orange juice for its different colors. Quibbling
                             jubilation.

Home was like his pockets—the displays of his nearly lyrical
                             life,
mechanical droppings, scattered cautiously throughout his
                             windowless rooms.
He was the unopened present in everyone's closet.
None but the cats preferred to see him
and his ancient Chinese maid was an okie.
She slept across the alley with the remnants of her love
                             -rubbing fat.
Her toilet was full of lilacs in tin cans which she ignored
and on her way to work she stepped on sleeping snails. She
                             was inadvertent.
The other was cut in half. Atlas without legs.
David standing on his groin. Mercury thumping on his torso
across whatever expanse eternity required. Congenital flotsam.
He'd cultivated the proper resentments but paid no attention
                             to promise or anxiety.
A compact, arrogant man, he went nude having nothing to hide.

In formaldehyde, in a preserve jar on a shelf in his closet,
were stored the replicas of his better half. He'd carved them
while waiting to die as a boy. "Not a shrine by any means,
just scrimshaw." He wouldn't bother now,

but if he'd carved them small enough to fit into a pouch,
he'd have worn the pouch around his neck.

His parents felt inclined
to offer palatial compensations once a month.

He dabbled in esoterica, breathless oriental frustrations, and
                                              the guitar.
His library was extensive. Each book flat on the floor,
in herringbone fashion, like bathroom tile. A dancer,
he never gardened, but hobbied frequently
with the rapturing shadows of his arms upon the wall.

No one knows why, but birds sometimes sing at midnight.

They both were three and a half feet tall, and out of
                                              circumstantial spite
had developed a convenient barrier of mutual trust. They felt
as rare to each other as the world felt to them. Neither
                                              remembered
how they met. Long since had origin been confused with secret
                                              ritual.

Specimens of accident or reminders of the truth,
there was no refuge, no preserve for them.
But, on special occasions once a month, they became a holiday
                                              of two.

The festival was at the hunchback's museum.
The ancient Chinese maid had been tutored to a sensual meal,
civilized, substantial, and punctuated by a rabid California
                                              wine.
She'd accented the decor with lilacs, two candles,
and set the chess set up near the dining board.

They both ached and took all day for granted.
Eight thirty. "Marvelous, marvelous, absolutely marvelous,"
the legless one said wheeling through the door,
"you look absolutely marvelous."
"Welcome, Mercury," the hunchback replied.

64

Maxims had never been this gay. Western music lapped through
the midden.
The hunchback ate with mannered concern. The legless one
indulged
with an obvious muscular candor. An Imperial undertaking!

Their monologues were abrupt, daring and inaccessible.
They disclosed themselves like matrons, hovering
over a chic conversation piece, divulging too much, which
meant nothing without the rest.
They were content, as they'd say, with together.

The ancient Chinese maid spend most of the evening in the
kitchen evicting cats. She left just before chess.
It was just a game and no one won. The legless one
had dropped a pawn near the finish and in reaching for it
upset the board and himself as well.

From under the table, the legless one laughed. Both laughed,
and laughed so hard, the hunchback tipped from his chair.
Face to face they laughed all the more.

Midnight. It rained—a wet, distended silence, brutal, comely
and precise.
An elderly crow blurted some visceral recriminations at a
dozing pack of sparrows below.

Under the table, locked hand in hand, not bothering with kisses,
the lovers emptied themselves into the middle of midnight,
for once like the rest—hardened keepers of necessity.

WORKSONGS FROM
THE SUICIDE TANK

I have dedicated these poems to my own natural death. A key to their moral and aesthetic motives can be found in Viktor Frankl's therapeutic technique of "paradoxical intention."

COUNTING SHEEP

How did it happen? When did it start?

Was it that time in New Hampshire
when Barbara's heart was so thin?
Was it in Portland that summer
I skipped and cracked my shin?
Or was it the first time I agreed with Paul
and dropped it all to patch up the mess in Minneapolis?
I can't recall; I've been so different ever since.

There was a moment, though, I know,
when pleasing as an aim became
too sweet an inconvenience to let go,
when it was smarter not to know the difference
between my heaven and their hell,
when I chose to decorate my soul for comfort
like a padded cell.

And now somehow my conscience
is the sum of my omissions.
And to think!
I would have died for them once
—under certain conditions.

It must have started when I came to see
that saints and honest senators
must have something up their sleeves,
that believing in tomorrow
is a tour de force to be endured
like savings bonds or slides of guided tours.

I used to think I'd sink if it weren't for that spare tire
I'd built up around my brain—but there's no security
even for the sane. After Barbara's hysterectomy
I got the gout; now, I use my phallus for a cane.

If I could just remember what I told myself that day,
play it back and lay the blame
—a time, a chance, a circumstance
would put reality to shame.

I've plagiarized my children, dissected by career,
answered all the questions I asked when I was six,
haven't meant my fun for years.
I've analyzed, apologized, taken classes at the U,
sponsored noble paper drives, creative cages at the zoo,
wooed the press with social graces
so they won't begrudge me my disgraces.

But Rip van Winkle is my patron saint.

I wake up every morning
with lipstick on my chin,
convinced I've lived my life
in a place I ve never been.

And I must be content
with projecting phantom compliments,
and settle for the peace that comes
like pantomime from proteges
who surely will remember *something*
to envy as sublime.
For nothing I'd do
would be enough
to redeem my manhood
from my successes.

I could treat myself to dirty girls,
wear wiglets drenched in prickly curls,
redress the world for millions
for mismarketing my mind;
but it's much too late to compensate
for a fate I can't believe is mine.

I will always be too old now
to die before my time.

QUESTIONS ON A MORAL AUTOPSY FORM

A Purgative Recital for Winfield Townley Scott

> ". . . If we are lucky/To live it out./If
> there is wisdom/Ever in envy/The only wisdom/
> Is to envy the old/Grown lean and tough/
> And wise with work/To the final night/Of
> the fulfilled year."
>
> —WTS

How was it? Was it hot,
            wind-worn and out of sorts,
            stupidly empty of stars,
the sky curling up like an ant
on a match,
            or was it frozen
            solid, clear to the end of light
that night you yawned
in epileptic desolation
            as your breath tipped over on the floor?
            Did your mind freeze up,
vapor lock: a lemon
fulfilling guarantees?
            had you said something better than anyone before
            with no one there to listen
then forget it? Was it your name, your name
you wore like a jew's tattoo, that you misplaced,
            fumbling through the campaign ribbons,
            affairs, the purple hearts for clues
night-blinded in your brain,
a gasp away from recognition,
            breathless: you
            who spoke love and dread
more fluently than breathing?

                    * * *

Why?

Why? Were you informally ignored? Too deep, they felt,
             for confidential chatter,
             too complex for wars?
But did they envy who you must have been
beneath it all so much
             your conscience couldn't bear
             to disappoint them anymore?

Or did you grieve to death
while growing up
             learning who you could have been
             was nothing but a lie?
Did you suspect the people

were enjoying you
             the way they do aquariums?
             Had you come to the age of indiscriminate disgust:
poetry and perjury
the only laxatives strong enough for love?
             Was Christmas this year
             a major triviality: the manger
so choked up with critics,
opera buffs, dilettante fanatics
             that you didn't feel at liberty
             to laugh?
Or was it when you caught yourself

screwing you behind your back
             more afraid of meaning
             than willing to admit yourself
without it?
Had they guessed you at charades the night before
             when they looked into your eyes
             and saw you mirrored in another's gaze:
that tom boy sparrow's perhaps,
caught napping on the wing,
             who crammed her beak
             back between her eyes
against your face mirrored in the window pane,

her soft bald head

                    drooling down the twilight
                    with the horror in your eyes?
Did your heart attack you in revenge
when it judged you had become
                    who you could not help but be
                    but never would have been
by choice?
Did you play yourself out
                    over too many moments
                    when there was nothing to do
but play dead?

                        * * *

Why? Why can't I leave your death alone?
          I feel I'm mongering my own instead of yours:
                    a young man whining
an old man's shame.
And I am.
          I'm guilty of professing you
                    corrupted into parody,
pandering your torments like an amateur
infatuated vulture, indiscreetly sharing
                    your innumerable last miles, teething,
                        by association, on my own denials.
I've bribed the hangman to watch you drop,
so you could show me how.

Granted, I'd identified with you
          but I know too much about defiance
                    to humiliate your ferocity
with sympathetic truths.
There was no compromise of destiny or conviction
          in the matter-of-fact fantastic risks you took
                    as a sympathizing alien, a spy in love
with a maniacally gifted land
blissfully atrocious as its people.
          This is no way to say I understand
                    the relentless candor of your dying
arrogantly, not quite by accident, so originally sincere.
Your death was no mistake.

I wanted so indignantly to cry,
      to praise you justified
         in claiming a rationale for tragedy
that I could stake my life on.
But I cannot condone what disappoints me:
      not that it's impossible to envy your demise,
         not that, but my exasperating disillusion
at finding no unusual excuses, not a single condescending lie,
only an insult to my passion, an intimidating honesty
      I cannot lament. Whether fulfilled by folly, wisdom,
         or by default, the vulgar truth: it makes no difference.
You didn't mind your death
at all.

ADVICE TO THE SELFLORN

So, you need to go morally nude, do you?
Free from roles and pretenses?
Goodhousekeeping deals and defenses?
A personal purist? Publically owned?
By your soul?! Oh come to your senses!
Roll over, conform! Perform
Like a clever consensus.
Be a little obscene, that's all they ask.
They wouldn't deign even to dream you
unless you were dressed correctly
in the latest corrective death mask.

You may recite who you are all you like,
Like a fable, a table of figures, or prayers.
But who can say
You've been what you've said?

Know thyself, if you wish to be known,
As a fiction of friends,
As hearsay at parties you've failed to attend.
There, on the tips of their tongues,
They say who you are
And, for everyone else but you, you are
Exactly what they have said.

Relax. You know who you'll be after you die.
They treat you as if you were already dead.

KOKOSCHKA'S DUMMY *

A Marriage Made in Heaven

Without pity, I picked her to love me forever,
more than no other man; breeding her always
out of my genius, mummied in arts,
a virgin hooker snagged on her rags.
　　　Obliged to bear all my secrets, to wear my life
like a habit, a hybrid of hopes and last chances,
in umbilical wounds like ideas she conceives
in chrysalis spastically scheming,
my navel her only eye.

　　　Five foot two, sweat like dew,
I will be my conception of you,
twin I am lost in, laboring lie
sweet as the odor of ice:
fruit of my spirit, my mistletoe crown,
fruit of the tree I am nailed to,
fruit of the tree I cut down.

　　　Beatrice was Dante's doll,
the doom-bearing bride of his muse.
　　　Merciful nurse, pillow, bedfellow,
naked as gold bleeding from lead, turning my mind
into my lover, replacing my life
with a mocking excuse not to die:
　　　you are that chaste and echoing well,
foundling among god's obsessions,
that wallowing place in the "depths of truth
where all disquiet drowns."

Ladies, schoolgirls, spinsters, and wives,
idols of the abyss I embrace, pregnant
as mirrors gazing on space, your passion
forges the flesh of god's mind,
but how can I tell you your hunger for me
I enticed is merely a fetish for hers I devised?

Dummy, darling, her mandate and fable,
my image and likeness is here in her hide,
conceived from a dead thing and so identified.

You may haunt through my sperm with your sorrow,
cuddle the faces into your cottonmouth eyes
but avoid my mystique,
garner your mysteries elsewhere;
don't toy with your meaning for me.
You can't tear me apart like a grapefruit
and shovel her out with my tool.
We portray each other too well.
Solace is our salvation.
Accomplices in our regrets,
our motive for love
is of course resignation.

She roves like dunes through my mind.
A libidinous bulge stitched in her stomach,
raving I prune her heart with my teeth;
ranting and swooning, wooing like worms
chewing homes in each other.
She's buried my seed in her stuffing.
I'm hatched in her box of wool,
her thighs rubbed raw and indented
wrapped around my spine.

Ladies, I scratch all the time,
crawl with her spirit, her claws
clenched in my lower intestines.
She's ladled me in through the runs in her soul,
sucks at my heart with her sex,
bites on my brain like a bullet
to keep from crying out
and stars rudely drain from my bowels
while trying to make an impression in you.

Miscellaneous ladies,
double your pity: husband your myths,
doll up your own approximations
—nothing but lovers

76

engendering truths from half lies.
　　Lose your own lives,
noosed in your halos, hooded in flesh
from the vast fishy thighs of ideals.
　　Doom is in the beholder.
I bear my genius with pride.

Venus picked me for her special one,
the apple of her eye,
fruit of the tree she is known by.
　　By instinct of death I seduced her,
conceived for her from my cunning
a bower of merciful pleasure,
a labor that took all my life.
　　Lovers in effigy,
how can I tell you my meaning?
I am that virgin place
where the angels go to die.

---

*Shot in the head and bayonated through the lung, but home from
the First World War, a young Oskar Kokoschka commissioned a
foreign seamstress to construct to his precise specifications a life-
sized female doll, a love fetish to be the exact replica of his anima.
Kokoschka wrote to the seamstress, in one of many letters accom-
panied by large, detailed drawings, "as I can bear no living people but
am often delivered into despair when alone, I beg you again to use
all your imagination, all your sensitiveness for the ghostly companion
you are preparing for me and to breathe into her such life that in the
end, when you have finished the body, there is no spot which does
not radiate feeling, to which you have not applied yourself to over-
come by the most complex devices the dead material. Then will all
the delicate and intimate gifts of nature displayed in the female body
be recalled to me in some desperate hour by some symbolic hiero-
glyph, or sign, with which you have secretly endowed that bundle of
rags." The Venus of Kokoschka was seen by his side at the Viennese
Opera, on shopping sprees, and at fashionable bistros. Seeking release
from a barren madness, he painted a full-breasted portrait of his
lover, (after making 160 preliminary drawings) and with her help
resurrected his art from the self of a dead thing. See Edith Hoffmann,
Kokoschka: His Life and Work (London, Faber and Faber, 1947.)

CHEATED AT SOLITAIRE

Responsible
for pleasure,
a native voyeur
meant to enjoy,
to be pleased,
to give meaning,
just so the world
won't perish alone
—all day
I witness the sky's immolation,
suffer my instincts
and testify,
promiscuously serene.

But the angels are bigots

and so are the trees,
and even my genes
have convenient amnesia.
The stars don't care
if I say them by heart,
savored
like deathbed confessions.

"As a man is, so he sees."

Only I
will be missing
when I die:
no more
than the values I seek,
the blood I share with the sea,
or the loveliness lost
in my body's debris.
Beauty
is a useless pretense,
a duty I use
to seem real.

My purpose offends me.

I worship the insult
and loudly
stare down the sun,
all the way down
through my brain
to learn why,
but I can't understand
the loneliness
in my eyes.

It's as if I'd already disappeared,

the tears in my veins, like memories,
weeping unsalvaged into the sand.
The sun is as blind as I am.

I might as well be a lion, owl, or rhino

not a man
that means what he sees.
All over my brain is the world,
but I, alone,
can hear what I say.
An echo,
jammed head down
inside my head,
I am nature
praising itself,
responsibly
self-deceived.

TOO MUCH TOO SOON

Hero in a magazine
diving from a yacht:

Faded and folded
into his brain
an image in flight
he dove from the plane
trying to be
what the others forgot.

But try as he might
to be what he thought,
he couldn't forget,
nor see what he sought
before it stained his shadow.

GENTLEMAN DADA

Let me be blunt. I am not a bad man.
Why not admit it? It's no secret anymore.

I do horrible things I am proud to abhor.
It's more than my right to do what I am:
pollution, pestilence, the baiting of pets,
provisional wars; what's more, my heart beats,
my ducts secrete in the dark; I eat and maim
with the same infallible nonchalance
for which I can take no credit.
Me and my hair-trigger whimsy!
Ooo how I wish those fabulous fliers
wouldn't use nets. Yet, my wife
banks on the fact that I'm kind.
And I am, in fact, pathologically kind
to toads, to patriot roses, cuddly swine.
I know nothing of wines. I can build the sublime
in half the time. I screw
with suave compassion. I really do.

But the ants?
Can the ants understand I'm not a bad man?
Can they possibly know how it feels?
Do they, for instance, record
the bushels of birdseed I've laid at their doors,
or chart the course of my shadow, build arks?
Do they wait philosophically for my spade?
I hope they do.
I hope they feel like I do
when I contemplate the news
and sigh when I come to their cities.
I hope they've taken the time
to enshrine in my backyard somewhere
a history of my deeds, some holy writ
and perhaps an idol
they curse and bite.

For better or worse, I am not a bad man.
It's more than my right to do what I am.

BACK TO THE DRAWING BOARD

Spiders darn my socks.
Generations of the butterfly
animate my clocks.
And I, in turn, mend time,

wedging my pulse into the crack,
stalling to keep forever intact,
the wind breaking
over my back,
my spine
spilling out my ass,
a broken hour glass.

Each Spring a little bit more is used up.

Fruit flies pollinate my dung.
Learned mockingbirds idealize my tongue.
And I obey my calling,

mating with bait to preserve the beginning,
methodically mounting my mind.
Defined by a function, like the rest,
a Midas brain I possess, a haunted node
itching with growths, a touchstone
potent with patents and spores;

the Angel of Spring is my master;

my mind: a motherlode of roses
fitted with dentures and diabolical tails,
of co-op lungs, geraniums crowned
with throny cerebrums, sunflowers petaled in nails.

I am the Victim's apprentice.

Time is at a critical mass.
I've paned my hothouse with magnifying glass.
And what I see
is instantly replaced with my identity.

I can't transcend the purpose I serve. In fact,
I'm unfit to survive it. But that's more humane
than what my conscience would have me endure.
And more secure.

One of Darwin's instructive darlings,
indulged discreetly, then decently killed for my facts,
the stations of apocalypse are coded in my genes.

In my wildest dreams I wouldn't have thought
my seman was part of a monstrous plot
to turn intelligence into a clock
—a zone, sterile of flesh,
where mind has a half-life all its own.

By loving and knowing all that we can,
we all serve the purpose of Entropy's plan.

A pretext for horror, and nothing more,
time is a context of bodies; and sex
an act of esprit de corps.

Dinosaurs, Dodos, Moas, and Man—what next?

POGROM UNDER THE TOUPEE

A Diagnostic Aberration for Wendy and Wombat

"Quite the contrary! It *is* a safe world now. Fail safe,
to be sure, now that we've succeeded. Can't you see?
Now, nothing's tainted with improbable unknowns.
You may have been a sainted-great-man long ago. But what's the use?
"We've conquered human nature—designed ourselves
with our own image and likeness in mind
and meet, infallibly, our greatest expectations.

"It's inconceivable, but we're convinced that you were spawned
through a schism in the Body Prophylactic;
an unspecified euphoria perhaps, a recalcitrant erotic act.
You're a throwback, a gruesome artifact of natural selection.

"We could have bottled you, you know, quite succinctly
before these pathologic inspirations began to fester so.
But the fact remains that you survived the intrauterine debacle
and disciplined your conscience to concentrate on you.

"The system's purity, you see, makes personality a moribund digression,
and in its wisdom, the legislature has decreed, as a popular priority,
the capture and display, or cure, of all psychological minorities.
Policy can't afford disorganized intelligence.
And the enterprise of privacy is demonstrably too costly.

"It's only a nothing-but world,
pasted over our hollow eyes,
and it's not polite
to poke around and stare.

"Thus, we must pronounce you, in this context, systematically insane.
In a word: infeasible,
and spreading, narcotic to our well-goomed generations.
Afflicted with a dreaded distemper of the ego,
besotted by dilemmas, deliberately occult,
you're a stigma, a malignant enigma, psycho-philosophically deformed.

"It's been proven that the organism must be seen, not heard,
if it's to gratify its longing for the feasibly absurd.
Relativity is wrong you see. It's too good to be true.
Anyway, this matter of intrinsics has been entirely surpassed
by a simply marvelous simplicity:
it's the naked grammar of it all, the voluptuous mechanics,
the economics of tranquillity, if you will.

"A place for every thing, and every thing in its place.
By thy syntax shall ye be known. But you,
you're not inclined to haircreams, dipilatories, schematic dreams.
You will not part your eyes.
You
are ill-defined,
uselessly unique, and pollute the very core of Christian Hygiene
with this selfish innocence, this cunning conscientious loneliness of yours.

"Who, for instance, could replace you if you disappeared?
Who, for law and records, could swab your spirit onto slides
or prescribe for you the appropriate, individualized delights?

"This decadent vitality is not a compromise.
It was complicity, after all, that led to these conclusions.
Your plight was handily deduced from statements pawned by peers,
dear ones overwrought by your inconvenient status.

"Inscrutable's the complaint. Quaint, perhaps, but insultingly elusive.
It's been rumored that you frequently ad lib, enthusiastically
withdraw from public piety and pranks,
harbor refuse, both inanimate and strange,
are sexually devoted to anatomical eccentrics.

"Diagnostically, you play too hard, know too much,
are maliciously serene.
You've victimized equality with freedom. In short,
we can't see through your fences, nor effectively throw stones.

"But take heart. Don't be blue. We can
omit you, if we choose, or renovate a way to rescue you.
We can program a postponement of this peevish prematurity

with a simple requisition for a surgical asylum
—not quite lobotomy, but rather a cordial transplantation.
with the measurably inane, wherein we ream your pith
of cosmic clatter, synchronize your will, drill a tiny well,
tap the irritating matter that makes your self so sudden, so incorrigibly
                                                                your own.
It's preventive therapy, my boy, sanitized dementia—jolly
as a mandatory binge, or maternal Sunday enemas.

"We'll just contort your style a little, make it worth your while,
weave a pattern in which worry has no value, engineer negotiable new vov
We'll make you free of contageous spontaneity,
compute for you a general, pre-experienced mystique,
install heroic quantities of noblizing shame. And in the end,
you will adore the organ,
substitute your secrets for lifetime avocations,
manage your contingencies for maximum composure.

"Gratified by yoyos, the statistically profound,
you will fantasize expediently
of festive rookeries and swine.

"Be reasonable!
Face the facts.
There is no room for you.
You have no other choice.
"You will move over!
We simply don't have time.
You must progress
to diplomatic contradictions,
be broken therapeutically,
or break."

86

MARGINALIA ON THE CUFF

of a Cynical Optimist in Quicksand

Vanished in finity, in gewgaws,
good service, and little girls,
Dante didn't sing to himself
but who can remember his jingle
after the refrain? And what does it matter
to the sea?

Aladdins without lamps,
we expect too much
from the marvelous
and fail to respect
our appearance:

Idol chances, poor risks,
unreasonably alive,
our sperm are fecund bullets
and our souls suspect our brains.
We all die the same: indignant
but reverently ashamed.

Fabulous!

and frail without a flaw
but our Christian cunning
with despair, itself
irrelevant as Justice,
we have staked our purpose on the mercy of our fear,
on our ingenious obeisance
to legitimate excuses, dreamed up
and deified long before our time
in colossal disappointment with infinity.

Mortality is too holy!

Yes, humanity is a tactless flattery,
a premature condolence,
bestowed upon the stones and silly crystals.
But, we are for free,
and it is our only strategy
to be imperative.

Preposterously sinister, god
is still a brave thing to say.
Valor is in the vanity.

But Dante should have saved his breath.
Life is not a consequence of Death.

By virtue of our gullible hypocrisy,
meaning and Death
must be divorced
to risk faith.
If you must die,
die vain
as dying without doubt.
Deliciously,
nothing but death is at stake.

Photo by Mark Acuff

Vincent Barrett Price is a reporter and columnist for THE NEW MEXICO INDEPENDENT in Albuquerque. A former Ford Foundation Fellow in anthropology, Price graduated from the University of New Mexico in 1962. He is married to artist Rini Price and has two sons, Jody and Keir, by a previous marriage. Price has published poetry in journals and reviews for the last 14 years both in this country and abroad. His first book of poems, THE CYCLOPS' GARDEN, was brought out in 1969 by the San Marcos Press. The poems in this volume were culled from three collections written between 1962 and 1971.

89